Identity Kit

An Anthology about Identity

PM Ruby Level

The PM Library is published by Thomson Learning Australia and is distributed as follows:

AUSTRALIA	NEW ZEALAND	UNITED KINGDOM
Thomson Learning	Nelson Price Milburn	Nelson Thornes
Level 7, 80 Dorcas Street	1 Te Puni Street	Delta Place
South Melbourne 3205	Petone	27 Bath Road
Victoria		Cheltenham GL53 7TH
		United Kingdom

First published in 2001
10 9 8 7 6 5 4 3
09 08 07 06

Text © Nelson Australia Pty Ltd 2001
Illustrations © Nelson Australia Pty Ltd 2001

Identity Kit: An Anthology about Identity
ISBN 1 86961 479 8

Designed by design rescue
Edited by Kate McGough
Cover illustration by Ian Forss
Photographs by Lindsay Edwards

Acknowledgements:
The publisher would like to acknowledge the following authors and publishers for their permission to reprint extracts from the titles below for this anthology:
'Brackets' by John Coldwell from *The Hutchinson Treasury of Children's Poetry*, 1988; *Bill's New Frock* by Anne Fine, Mammoth, London, 1999; *Toad Rage* by Morris Gleitzman, Puffin, Australia, 1999; *Chinese Cinderella–The Secret Story of an Unwanted Daughter* by Adeline Yen Mah, Puffin, Australia, 1999; *Gilbert's Ghost Train* by David Metzenthen, Scholastic Press, Australia, 1997; 'Me I Am!' by Jack Prelutsky from *The Walker Book of Poetry*, Walker Books, London, 1983; 'Truth' by Barrie Wade from *One Hundred Years of Poetry for Children*, Oxford University Press, London; *Charlotte's Web* by E.B. White, Hamish Hamilton, 1952.
The publishers acknowledge the assistance of **Desley Roy** in the selection of material for this anthology.

Every effort has been made to trace and acknowledge copyright, but in some cases we have been unsuccessful. The publishers apologise for any accidental infringement and welcome information to redress the situation.

Printed in China by 1010 Printing International Limited

This title is published under the imprint of Nelson School.
Nelson Australia Pty Limited ACN 058 280 149 (incorporated in Victoria) trading as Thomson Learning Australia.

Contents

ME I AM!	4
Toad Rage	6
Acting Up	12
Chinese Cinderella	20
(Brackets)	34
Charlotte's Breakfast	36
The Same but Different	40
The Problem with Dally	50
Truth	56
Bill's New Frock	58

ME I AM!

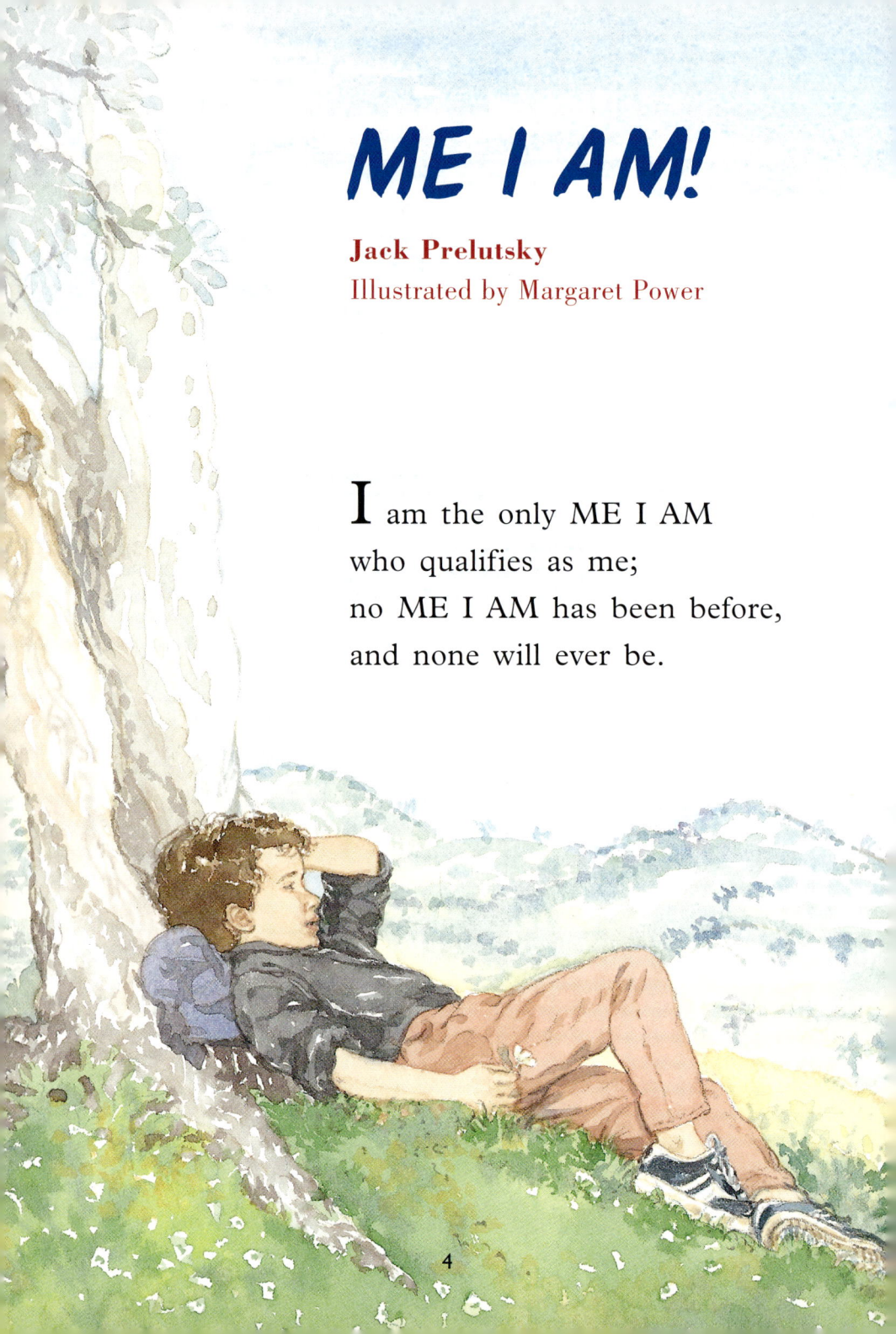

Jack Prelutsky
Illustrated by Margaret Power

I am the only ME I AM
who qualifies as me;
no ME I AM has been before,
and none will ever be.

No other ME I AM can feel
the feelings I've within;
no other ME I AM can fit
precisely in my skin.

There is no other ME I AM
who thinks the thoughts I do;
the world contains one ME I AM,
there is no room for two.

I am the only ME I AM
this earth shall ever see;
that ME I AM I always am
is no one else but ME!

Toad Rage

Morris Gleitzman Illustrated by Ian Forss

Setting the Scene

The Sydney 2000 Olympic Games aren't far away. Limpy and his cousin, Goliath, are determined to bring honour and respect to all cane toads in Australia — by becoming fluffy Olympic mascots.

But it's not that easy. How do you make humans love you? Especially when humans think cane toads are the ugliest creatures on earth. And why do humans think some animals are more important than others?

'Go on,' said the voice. 'Don't be embarrassed.'

A kangaroo was dabbing its eyes with a tissue and holding a couple more out to Limpy and Goliath.

'No thanks,' said Goliath.

'It's OK to be upset,' said the kangaroo. 'I would be if I'd just discovered I was an unloved species.'

'We're not upset,' said Goliath menacingly to the kangaroo. 'And we're not unloved. I love my cousin Limpy and he loves me.'

Limpy nodded. But only for a moment because he was feeling so upset.

The kangaroo was right.

How could I have been so stupid, thought Limpy miserably. How could I have imagined I could have a real friendship with a human? How could I think humans would want to make a fluffy toy out of me?

'Sorry,' the kangaroo was saying. 'Didn't mean to rub it in. If it makes you feel any better, imagine what it's like for me. Humans love me. I'm on the Australian coat of arms. And every travel show ever made about this country. Plus most of the cooking shows. Imagine how I felt when the Games Mascot Committee gave me the thumbs down.'

Identity Kit

The kangaroo blew its nose loudly on a tissue.

A koala put its arm round the kangaroo. 'I know how you feel, mate,' it said, and took a swig from a bottle.

'At least they didn't try and swat you,' said a blowfly indignantly.

'Or rush out of the room screaming,' said a diamond-bellied black snake sadly.

'Or scratch you off the list,' said a flea bitterly.

'I wouldn't be a mascot now if they came on their hands and knees and begged,' said a funnel-web spider. 'Not after all the unkind things they said about me in that committee room.'

'At least they said them to your face,' said a crocodile. 'All I got was a letter.'

'I wouldn't be a mascot now if they offered me a million dollars,' said a wombat.

'I wouldn't be one,' said a blue-tongued lizard, 'if they offered me a million carports with cracks in the foundations big enough to raise a family in.'

'I wouldn't be one if they offered me a million sticks of sugar cane,' said a cane beetle.

'Or a million sticks,' said Goliath, snatching a tissue and blowing his nose.

Identity Kit

Limpy listened to the hurt, indignant voices of the animals and insects around him, and suddenly he felt his warts prickling with anger.

'What I reckon,' he said, 'is that we've all been treated shabbily by our country.'

The other animals and insects fell silent.

They turned to look at Limpy.

'These Games,' continued Limpy, his voice ringing off the wet walls, 'are meant to be about a universal spirit of friendship. That's what they're always saying on telly. Well, the humans haven't shown us much friendship. I reckon we're better off not being a part of such an unfriendly Games. When we look back at all this, I reckon we won't have to feel sad for one minute about not being mascots.'

The animals and insects looked at him, eyes shining.

Then they all burst into mournful cries.

'Yes, we will,' wailed a fruit bat. 'We'll feel sad and worthless for the rest of our lives.'

(Extract taken from *Toad Rage* by Morris Gleitzman, Puffin, Australia 1999)

Acting Up

Sally Morrell   Photographs by Lindsay Edwards

HOW DO YOU BECOME ANOTHER PERSON — ESPECIALLY WHEN YOU ARE STILL LEARNING ABOUT THE PERSON YOU ARE?

Eleven-year-old Nathan Derrick does it all the time. As a professional actor, he has to become someone else every time he takes on a new job.

Nathan has played many different roles — from a polite, well-behaved Austrian schoolboy in the musical *The Sound of Music* to a filthy young thief in the musical *Les Miserables*.

"It's not really that hard to be someone else," Nathan says.

But, he admits, it takes a bit of homework to make a character look believable to the audience.

Acting Up

"You don't just go on stage and become that person without having to think about who that person is," he says. "You have to work out who they are and try to understand them so you can then be them as an actor."

Nathan says he was taught the 'Who, What, Where, When, Why and How' approach to acting by one of his directors and it has always worked with him.

"First, I sit down and think about who the character is and what they are doing in the musical or the play," he says. "Then I think about the setting of the musical or play. *The Sound of Music* was set in Austria in 1938, so I learned about that time. Then I thought about why my character says things, and how and why my character acts the way he does."

Nathan discusses the 'Who, What, Where, When, Why and How' approach to acting.

Identity Kit

"I was playing Kurt, one of the children, so we talked about how all the children were pretty well-behaved and stuff. It helped us all get into character," Nathan says.

As part of their on-the-job schooling by a tutor, the children also did a project on their character.

"That helped as well. I had to give my character a real-life history, as if I was telling his story," Nathan says.

"I had to think about when Kurt would have been born and what his life would have been like. It was good because it helped Kurt become real."

Everyone in the musical was called by his or her character's name during the six-week rehearsal time and for the length of the musical run.

"Other people in the cast called me Kurt. I called my friend Emily, Brigitta, and my friend, Maddy, Gretel. That way we could feel like a family and relate to each other like brothers and sisters," he says.

But Nathan says he didn't feel that Kurt, his character, was taking over too much of his life.

Acting Up

"Oh, no, once I got in the car to go home I was back to being Nathan again. Kurt didn't take over, it was just a way for all of us to get into our characters," he says.

Nathan and his signed poster from *The Sound of Music*.

Nathan (middle row, second from left) and other cast members from *The Sound of Music*.

Nathan continued going to school during the run of performances but often left mid-morning for a matinee, or after lunch so he could sleep before that night's performance.

"But I didn't mind not being around that much. I don't really like going to school," he says.

And that's not because he finds the work hard — even with the missed hours, he tries to keep up with all his schoolwork. It's just that his classmates haven't been very supportive of his chosen career.

"I don't have many friends at school. My best friend, Eammon, is also an actor, but he goes to another school," he says.

"The kids at school either ignore it all or ignore me. It's pretty mean, but I'm used to it by now."

Even when Nathan made the front page of the city newspaper, no one at school mentioned it, not even the teachers.

"I think Mum and Dad get more upset than I do. They get hurt for me, but I don't let it bother me that much," he says. "But I reckon if I was on the front page because I could run fast or was good at football, it wouldn't be like this."

Nathan wants to continue acting and singing when he leaves school.

"My younger brother, Brodie, started acting and I sort of followed him into it. I found I really liked it," he says.

His first big production was playing the young Peter Allen in *The Boy from Oz*, the musical biography of the famous Australian entertainer. Nathan was nine-years-old at the time.

"I learnt a lot from that. At first I wasn't sure how you went about being someone else but I watched a whole lot of videos of Peter Allen and tried to learn about him," he says.

Identity Kit

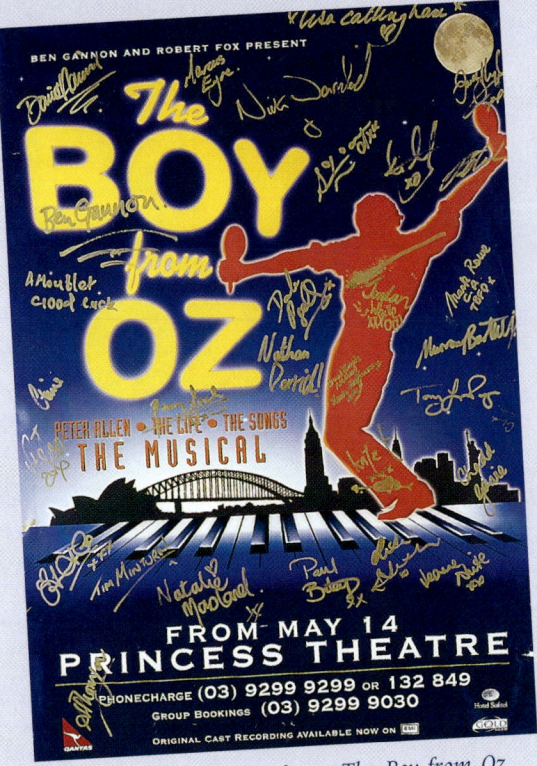

Nathan's signed poster from The Boy from Oz.

"The director told me the most important thing was to enjoy myself and to have fun, and that was great," he says.

Nathan really enjoyed himself. So much so that, when *The Boy from Oz* ended, he felt desperately unhappy.

"It was *really* hard. I missed the friends I had made, I missed the music and I missed being the character," he says.

Nathan became so depressed that his parents worried about him. But before long, *The Sound of Music* came up and kept him busy for almost half a year.

"When that finished it was also really hard, but this time I was more ready for it," he says.

To keep busy, Nathan took a role in an amateur production of the French musical *Les Miserables*. He played the dirty little thief, Gavroche, who lives alone on the streets of Paris in the years leading up to the French Revolution.

"It's quite a change from Kurt, but that's good. This time I'm a really bad character. I carry knives and I give a lot of cheek. Gavroche has even killed dogs for food!" he says.

Nathan says the most important thing about being an actor is to enjoy what you are doing. It's also important not to get too caught up in 'acting' as your character.

"Basically, you should have fun and be yourself. You have to act as your character, but you have to make it believable. You have to be natural," he says.

"If you've done all the work before-hand, thinking about who you are as the character, then you shouldn't have to 'act' — you should just be natural."

Nathan bought Ozzie, his golden retriever, with his earnings from *The Boy from Oz*.

Chinese Cinderella

Adeline Yen Mah   Illustrated by Xiangyi Mo

Adeline Yen Mah's mother died while giving birth to her. From that moment, Adeline's family considered her bad luck. Chinese Cinderella *is the story of Adeline's struggle to prove her worth and value to a family that barely acknowledges her at all.*

Setting the Scene

It's 1941, and the young Adeline (Wu Mei) lives with her family in Tianjin, a city port on the north coast of China. She has just started school and has been awarded a medal for topping her class during the week.

Chinese Cinderella

Characters

Ye Ye

Nai Nai

Father

Niang

Aunt Baba

Big Brother

Second Brother

Third Brother

Fourth Brother

Big Sister

Adeline
(Wu Mei)

Little Sister

Identity Kit

The dinner-bell rang at seven. Aunt Baba took my hand and led me into the dining-room.

I went to the foot of the table and sat at my assigned seat between Second Brother and Third Brother as my three brothers ran in, laughing and jostling each other. I cringed as Second Brother sat down on my right. He was always saying mean things to me and grabbing my share of goodies when nobody was looking.

Chinese Cinderella

Second Brother used to sit next to Big Brother but the two of them fought a lot. Father finally separated them when they broke a fruit bowl fighting over a pear.

Big Brother winked at me as he sat down. He had a twinkle in his eye and was whistling a tune. Yesterday he'd tried to teach me how to whistle but no matter how hard I tried I couldn't make it work. Was Big Brother up to some new mischief today?

Identity Kit

Last Sunday afternoon, I came across him crouched by Grandfather Ye Ye's bed, watching him like a cat while Ye Ye took his nap. A long black hair from Ye Ye's right nostril was being blown out and drawn in with every snore. Silently but swiftly, Big Brother suddenly approached Ye Ye and carefully pinched the nasal hair between his forefinger and thumb. There was a tantalising pause as Ye Ye exhaled with a long, contented wheeze. Meanwhile I held my breath, mesmerised and not daring to make a sound.

Finally, Ye Ye inhaled deeply. Doggedly, Big Brother hung on. The hair was wrenched from its root. Ye Ye woke up with a yell, jumped from his bed, took in the situation with one glance and went after Big Brother with a feather duster.

Laughing hysterically, Big Brother rushed out of the room, slid down the banister and made a clean getaway into the garden, all the time holding Ye Ye's hair aloft like a trophy.

Chinese Cinderella

Third Brother took his seat on my left. His lips were pursed and he was trying to whistle unsuccessfully. Seeing the medal on my uniform, he raised his eyebrow and smiled at me. 'What's that?' he asked.

    'It's an award for topping my class. My teacher says I can wear it for seven days.'

    'Congratulations! First week at school and you get a medal! Not bad!'

While I was basking in Third Brother's praise, I suddenly felt a hard blow across the back of my head. I turned around to see Second Brother glowering at me.

'What did you do *that* for?' I asked angrily.

Deliberately, he took my right arm under the table and gave it a quick, hard twist while no one was looking. 'Because I feel like it, that's why, you ugly little squirt! This'll teach you to show off your medal!'

Identity Kit

I turned for help from Third Brother but he was looking straight ahead, obviously not wishing to be involved. At that moment, Father, Niang and Big Sister came in together and Second Brother immediately let go of my arm.

Niang was speaking to Big Sister in English and Big Sister was nodding assent. She glanced at all of us smugly as she took her seat between Second Brother and Niang, full of her own self-importance at being so favoured by our stepmother. Because her left arm had been paralysed from a birth injury, her movements were slow and awkward and she liked to order me, or Third Brother, to carry out her chores.

'Wu Mei (Fifth Younger Sister)!' she now said. 'Go fetch my English–Chinese dictionary. It's on my bed in my room. Niang wants me to translate something…'

Chinese Cinderella

I was halfway off my chair when Nai Nai said, 'Do the translation later! Sit down, Wu Mei. Let's have dinner first before the dishes get cold. Here, let me first pick a selection of soft foods to send up to the nursery so the wet nurse can feed the two youngest …' She turned to Niang with a smile. 'Another two years and all seven grandchildren will be sitting around this table. Won't that be wonderful?'

Identity Kit

Niang's two-year-old son, Fourth Brother, and her infant daughter, Little Sister, were still too young to eat with us. However, they were already 'special' from the moment of their birth. Though nobody actually said so, it was simply understood that everyone considered Niang's 'real' children to be better-looking, smarter, and simply superior in every way to Niang's stepchildren. Besides, who dared disagree?

For dessert, the maids brought in a huge bowl of my favourite fruit, dragons' eyes! I was so happy I couldn't help laughing out loud.

Nai Nai gave us each a small bowl of fruit and I counted seven dragons' eyes in mine. I peeled off the leathery brown skin and was savouring the delicate white flesh when Father suddenly pointed to my medal.

'Is this medal for topping your class?' he asked.

I nodded eagerly, too excited to speak. A hush fell upon the table. This was the first time anyone could remember Father singling me out or saying anything to me. Everyone looked at my medal.

'Is the left side of your chest heavier?' Father continued, beaming with pride. 'Are you tilting?'

I flushed with pleasure and could barely swallow. My big Dia Dia was actually teasing me! On his way out, he even patted me on my head. Then he said, 'Continue studying hard and bringing honour to our Yen family name so we can be proud of you.'

All the grown-ups beamed at me as they followed Father out of the room. How wonderful! I must study harder and keep wearing this medal so I can go on pleasing Father, I thought to myself.

But what was this? Big Sister was coming towards me with a scowl. Without a word, she reached over and snatched two dragons' eyes from my bowl as she left the room. My three brothers followed her example. Then they all ran out, leaving me quite alone with my silver medal, staring at my empty bowl.

(Extract from *Chinese Cinderella – The Secret Story of an Unwanted Daughter* by Adeline Yen Mah, Puffin, Australia, 1999)

Adeline (Wu Mei) finished her schooling in England. She studied medicine in London and immigrated to the United States where she practised as a physician for twenty-six years. She is now an internationally successful writer.

(Brackets)

John Coldwell   Illustrated by Melissa Webb

It was Wednesday. Maths. Page 28.
And I was already thinking about tomorrow.
Thursday. Maths. Page 29.

We were doing problems.
The ones where you have to remove the brackets first.

I was on question 13 and right inside a bracket,
When this strange phrase came into my head.
And before I could trap it in a bracket
It shot out of my mouth
Into the classroom.

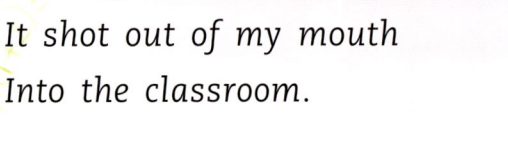

"Bring on the dancing prunes!"

The room went silent
And thirty pairs of bracket-solving eyes
Swivelled in my direction.
The teacher stopped putting crosses
In somebody's maths book
And looked crossly at me.
"What did you say?"

I could have told him
But instead,
I put a bracket round my reply
And said
"Nothing."

The teacher sighed.
"How would it be if **everybody**
Called out the first thing that came into their heads?"
(Very interesting.)

Charlotte's Breakfast

E.B. White   Illustrated by Rob Mancini

'Watch me wrap up this fly.'

A fly that had been crawling along Wilbur's trough had flown up and blundered into the lower part of Charlotte's web and was tangled in the sticky threads. The fly was beating its wings furiously trying to break loose and free itself.

'First,' said Charlotte, 'I dive at him.' She plunged headfirst towards the fly. As she dropped, a tiny silken thread unwound from her rear end.

Charlotte's Breakfast

'Next, I wrap him up.' She grabbed the fly, threw a few jets of silk round it, and rolled it over and over, wrapping it so that it couldn't move. Wilbur watched in horror. He could hardly believe what he was seeing, and although he detested flies he was sorry for this one.

'There!' said Charlotte. 'Now I knock him out, so he'll be more comfortable.' She bit the fly. 'He can't feel a thing now,' she remarked. 'He'll make a perfect breakfast for me.'

Identity Kit

'You mean you *eat* flies?' gasped Wilbur.

'Certainly. Flies, bugs, grasshoppers, choice beetles, moths, butterflies, tasty cockroaches, gnats, midgets, daddy-long-legs, centipedes, mosquitoes, crickets—anything that is careless enough to get caught in my web. I have to live, don't I?'

'Why, yes, of course,' said Wilbur. 'Do they taste good?'

'Delicious. Of course, I don't really eat them. I drink them—drink their blood. I love blood,' said Charlotte, and her pleasant, thin voice grew even thinner and more pleasant.

'Don't say that!' groaned Wilbur. 'Please don't say things like that!'

'Why not? It's true, and I have to say what is true. I am not entirely happy about my diet of flies and bugs, but it's the way I'm made. A spider has to pick up a living somehow or other, and I happen to be a trapper. I just naturally build a web and trap flies and other insects. My mother was a trapper before me. Her mother was a trapper before her. All our family have been trappers. Way back for thousands and thousands of years we spiders have been laying for flies and bugs.'

'It's a miserable inheritance,' said Wilbur, gloomily. He was sad because his new friend was so bloodthirsty.

(Extract taken from *Charlotte's Web* by E. B. White, Hamish Hamilton, 1952)

The Same, but Different

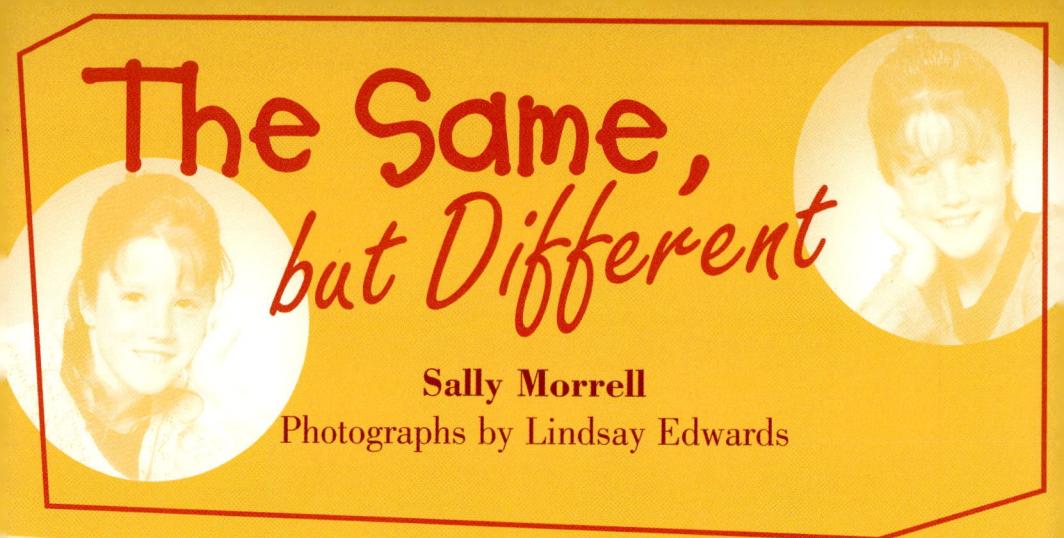

Sally Morrell
Photographs by Lindsay Edwards

Identical twins Ashleigh and Caitlin Roberts have very different views about what it's like to look exactly the same as someone else.

"I really like looking like Ashleigh. I just like being like her," says Caitlin.

But Ashleigh doesn't like being a twin. "I don't like looking the same as someone else all the time. I'd much rather look different," she says. "People say all the time, 'Oh, I'd love to be a twin,' but I don't like it at all. I'd want to have Cait as my sister but I'd rather not be a twin."

> "I really like looking like Ashleigh. I just like being like her."

The Same, but Different

Caitlin says she feels special being a twin. "It's not just looking the same that I like, it's also having someone to play with when you get home and when you go away. I just really love being a twin," she says.

> "I'd much rather look different... I'd want to have Cait as my sister but I'd rather not be a twin."

Identity Kit

Caitlin doesn't mind that Ashleigh doesn't like being a twin as much as she does. "It doesn't bother me, really. She's always felt that way," she says.

The 10-year-old twins are indeed a mirror image of each other. They both have long brown hair, the same brown eyes and the same wide smile. The only difference is the pattern of freckles that dots their noses. But you would have to be right up close to them to be able to work out who was who.

Ashleigh says that even in their own family, not everyone can tell them apart.

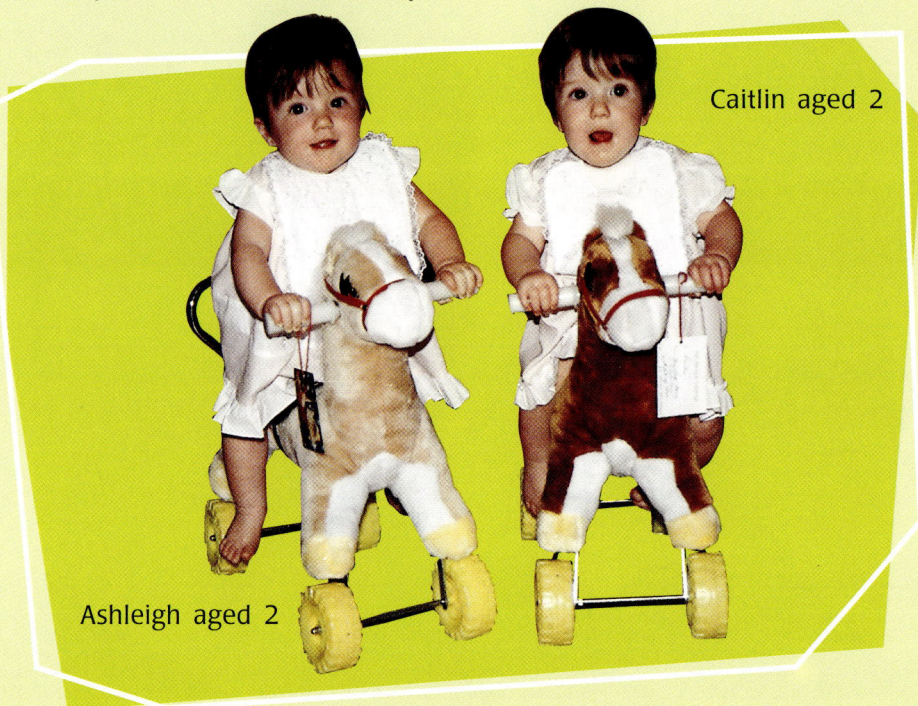

Caitlin aged 2

Ashleigh aged 2

The Same, but Different

Even in their own family, not everyone can tell them apart

"Mum always can. I don't know how she does it but she does, even when we have our backs turned. Dad still can't tell us apart most of the time," Ashleigh says. "Sometimes he gets it right, but usually he can't tell the difference. It doesn't matter to me."

But it matters to Caitlin. "You can tell sometimes he's just guessing. I guess I'm used to it, but it does still bother me a bit. I get a bit annoyed," she says.

Their eight-year-old brother, Christopher, gets it right almost all the time but the twins say their dog, Kelsey, is never wrong.

"She bites Ash sometimes but she never bites me. She must be able to tell the difference," says Caitlin.

Identity Kit

When Caitlin and Ashleigh started school, they both had to wear the same uniform. Teachers and students couldn't tell them apart.

"Everyone kept getting us mixed up all the time. I didn't like it," says Ashleigh.

After two years of being in the same class, the girls wanted a change. They asked to be separated, at least for one year to give it a try.

"It's great," says Ashleigh. "I don't want to be in the same class again."

Caitlin says that while it was annoying that the other children and the teachers mixed them up, she really didn't mind that much. She would even be happy to share a class with her sister again.

"But we won't be in the same class again," Ashleigh insists. "Mum's promised."

Caitlin has lots of friends at school.

The Same, but Different

Before they went into different classes, the girls preferred to play with each other. But once they went their separate ways, they started making new friends.

Ashleigh became especially close to Bree, a new girl at the school.

"When Bree arrived at the school, I had to show her around and she liked playing with me and I liked playing with her. Since then we've been best friends," Ashleigh says.

While Caitlin has lots of friends at school, she has no special friend. "Ash is my best friend," she says.

Ashleigh knows that Caitlin and Bree aren't good friends, but she says it doesn't worry her. "Bree says Caitlin is different to me. I can't help that," she says.

Ashleigh became especially close to Bree.

Identity Kit

Caitlin admits it makes her sad that she is no longer her sister's best friend. "I'm disappointed it happened," she says. "But I've talked about it with Mum. Anyway, there's not much I can do about it."

But Caitlin has made many other new friends who are not in the same group as Bree and Ashleigh.

"It's nice because they can tell us apart. It's easier because they always know who I am. And my friends have a lot of sleepovers but Ashleigh hasn't been invited to a sleepover yet," she says.

Caitlin is the most determined.

You would think that because the girls look exactly the same they would have similar personalities but they don't. For while Caitlin is the more reserved of the twins, she is also the most determined.

Ashleigh is very outgoing and it doesn't seem like she would ever be bothered by much. Caitlin is quieter and is very particular about what she likes and doesn't like. She has always taken care with her appearance but Ashleigh is only just starting to get interested in hairstyles and clothes.

The twins also never dress the same, even by accident.

"We go separately when we go with Mum to buy clothes. That way we won't buy the same things or, I guess, want to buy the same things," says Ashleigh. "But we always come back with different things anyway. I guess we have different tastes."

Ashleigh is very outgoing.

Identity Kit

Caitlin was the bigger baby and was always slightly bigger than her sister. Now, Ashleigh is one size bigger in shoes, a centimetre taller and a little heavier than her sister.

Even though Ashleigh would rather not have been born a twin, she says it does have its advantages.

QUICK QUESTIONS

Name: Caitlin Roberts

What is your favourite colour?
Lime Green

What is your favourite food?
Capsicum

Do you have a hero? Who is she/he and why?
Cathy Freeman — I like to run!

What is your favourite music group/singer?
Anastasia

What is your favourite book?
What Kind of Friend Are You? by Lauren Day.

What is your favourite game?
Twister

What is your favourite animal?
Dog

The Same, but Different

"Well, there's always someone to play with. When you get home from school, when you go away for holidays, you always have someone there to play with. Last time we went to the beach, we could boogie-board together. I like that," she says.

"I love it," says Caitlin.

QUICK QUESTIONS

Name: Ashleigh Roberts

What is your favourite colour?
Yellow

What is your favourite food?
Bananas

Do you have a hero? Who is she/he and why?
Cathy Freeman — I want to be a runner when I grow up.

What is your favourite music group/singer?
Five

What is your favourite book?
The Seven Little Australians by Ethel Turner

What is your favourite game?
Monopoly

What is your favourite animal?
Dog

The Problem with Dally

David Metzenthen   Illustrated by Jenny Mountstephen

Things have changed so much for Martin Dean and his family lately. His younger brother, Dally, is dying of leukemia. Dally's illness places a lot of pressure on Martin. Some days, it seems too much to cope with. Some days, Martin doesn't know how to feel or act.

Setting the Scene

Martin is taking Carl, Dally's dog, for a long walk. He stops and sits on a log, and thinks about Dally. These days, Dally is all Martin ever thinks about.

The Problem with Dally

I sit on my log and think back. Dally's sickness has been like a long journey our whole family has been on. And that journey has been interrupted by many things. Including me losing my temper a lot.

I didn't even know I had a bad temper until Dally was sick. Now I seem to be in a bad mood most of the time. My bad moods build up and up, then bingo! Or bang. I've been in fights. I was sent off the footy field for Unduly Rough Play. I also copped heaps for swearing at Mr Hendry, a student teacher.

The pressure of Dally being sick never stops. For instance, I had to come home early from a school camp. And I always have to be quiet and keep the television turned down. I also have to be polite to anybody who asks about Dally. And I have to listen to the kid crying. And I have to think about what is happening to him all the time. And I have to know just how many tablets and injections he has, and I have to put up with people coming to the house every day. I even feel guilty when I laugh, even when it might only be at Kramer on 'Seinfeld'. Everything is getting to me.

And when I hear the word 'death' I get a feeling like a kick in the stomach. And when I ride past the cemetery I almost collapse. When I see ambulances, a funeral car, a dead animal—man! All this pressure just adds up. I'm like a tyre about to have a blow-out.

Or I was.

Identity Kit

In the last day or two I think I must've developed a puncture. My bad mood has lost its badness. I'm too tired to fight or get aggro. My anger has fizzled away. I feel flat as a pancake and twice as floppy.

Man, I do want to get angry at what's happening to Dally—but now I simply don't have the energy. All my strength goes into thinking. Unfortunately, all this thinking hasn't got me too far. I want answers to serious questions and I want them now!

The Problem with Dally

Why can't Dally be fixed? Why did he get sick in the first place? What's really happening to him? Will he be here another day? Another week? Another month? Another year?

No-one can answer this stuff. I know that and it makes me feel even more useless. What can I do? Nothing, except stick around.

OK, so stick around I will. I never really was going to run away, like I said before. It was just a thought.

(Extract taken from *Gilbert's Ghost Train* by David Metzenthen, Scholastic Press, Australia, 1997)

Truth

Barrie Wade   Illustrated by Anna Wilson

Sticks and stones may break my bones,
but words can also hurt me.
Stones and sticks break only skin,
while words are ghosts that haunt me.

Slant and curved the word-swords fall
to pierce and stick inside me.
Bats and bricks may ache through bones,
but words can mortify me.

Pain from words has left its scar
on mind and heart that's tender.
Cuts and bruises now have healed;
it's words that I remember.

You're wrong
You're stupid
I don't like you
You're weird
Go away!
You'll never amount to anything

Bill's New Frock

Anne Fine   Illustrated by Tom Jellett

Much to Bill Simpson's horror, he wakes up one morning to find he has turned into a girl. And no one seems to have noticed the change. His parents and school friends act as though nothing is different, as if he'd been a girl all his life.

Bill doesn't know how or why it happened. He's pretty sure he isn't dreaming and there isn't much he can do about it. But things get even worse — Bill's mum makes him wear a dress to school.

Bill only becomes a girl for one day — without explanation, he turns back into a boy that night. But one day as a girl is enough for Bill to experience a totally different side to life.

Setting the Scene

Bill's classmates are settling down to do some school work. But Bill can't concentrate. Not only has he become a girl, but he's the only girl in class wearing a dress.

Bill's New Frock

Characters

Bill

Mrs Collins

Flora

Kirsty

Nick

Philip

Talilah

Identity Kit

Back in the classroom, everyone settled down at their tables.

'We'll do our writing first, shall we?' said Mrs Collins. 'And after that, we'll reward ourselves with a story.'

While Mrs Collins handed out the writing books and everyone scrabbled for pencils and rubbers, Bill looked around his table.

He was the only one in a dress.

Flora was wearing trousers and a blue blouse. Kirsty and Nick were both wearing jeans and a shirt. Philip was wearing corduroy slacks and a red jumper, and Talilah wore bright red satin bloomers under her fancy silk top.

Yes, there was no doubt about it. Talilah looked snazzy enough to go dancing, but Bill was the only one in a frock.

Oh, this was awful! What on earth had happened? Why didn't anybody seem to have noticed? What could he do? When would it end?

Identity Kit

Bill Simpson put his head in his hands, and covered his eyes.

'On with your work down there on table five,' warned Mrs Collins promptly.

She meant him. He knew it. So Bill picked up his pen and opened his books. He couldn't help it. He didn't seem to have any choice. Things were still going on in their own way, as in a dream.

He wrote more than he usually did. He wrote it more neatly than usual too. If you looked back through the last few pages of his work, you'd see he'd done a really good job, for him.

But you wouldn't have thought so, the way Mrs Collins went on when she saw it.

'Look at this,' she scolded, stabbing her finger down on the page. 'This isn't very neat, is it? Look at this dirty smudge. And the edge of your book looks as if it's been *chewed*!'

She turned to Philip to inspect his book next. It was far messier than Bill's. It was more smudgy and more chewed-looking. The writing was untidy and irregular. Some of the letters were so enormous they looked like giants herding the smaller letters haphazardly across the page.

Identity Kit

'Not bad at all, Philip,' she said. 'Keep up the good work.'

Bill could scarcely believe his ears. He was outraged. As soon as she'd moved off, he reached out for Philip's book, laid it beside his own on the table, and compared the two.

'It isn't fair!' he complained bitterly. 'Your page is *much* worse than my page. She didn't say anything nice to *me*.'

Philip just shrugged and said:

'Well, girls are neater.'

Bill felt so cross he had to sit on his hands to stop himself from thumping Philip.

(Extract taken from *Bill's New Frock* by Anne Fine, Mammoth, London, 1999)